METAMORPHOSIS

A PROPHETIC WORD ABOUT RADICAL CHANGE IN 2018

BY JENNIFER LECLAIRE
BY BEST-SELLING AUTHOR OF
THE MAKING OF A PROPHET

TABLE OF CONTENTS

CHAPTER 1
A METAMORPHOSIS IS UNDERWAY

"I will bring the change I've promised, first little by little and then an outward manifestation of an inner working I have been doing in My people."

Relaxing in one of Jim Bakker's condos the morning after a July 2017 marathon filming session for his show, I pondered and prayed about the coming days. With a live band practicing loudly in the studio space below my balcony, I heard the Lord say one attention-demanding word, "metamorphosis."

I've learned when the Lord speaks a single word in that oh-so-familiar still small voice, He always has more on His mind. He pauses because He wants us to press into His heart to hear the rest of the story. He craves an ever-increasingly intimate relationship with us, so at times He whispers one word in our ear to stir a hunger in our heart to lean in a little closer.

Understanding the ways of God, I quieted my soul and prayed. The music from the band below grew dim as if I was in another dimension. Soon enough, I heard the Lord say, "You've been through a metamorphosis. You're a new creature."

I held on to those words, pondering, processing and praying for months. I knew it was not just a personal word, as I am often a forerunner for the prophetic messages the Lord releases to me and through me.

In the months ahead, I experienced a growing prophetic sense 2018 would be a year of great growth on many fronts. God-hungry people will grow. Christ-centered churches that allow Holy Spirit His liberty will grow. Kingdom-minded businesses will grow.

As I continued meditating on this "metamorphosis" word and prophetic sensing of great growth I got another revelation: You cannot see growth without a metamorphosis. Indeed, growth—whether spiritual or natural—is demands change. Growth is a process. It happens in stages. It's progressive.

For me, it was the best of times and it was the worst of times. Maybe you can relate. The painful metamorphosis I experienced in the first half of 2017 started bearing exponential fruit in the second half of the same year—and I know this is just the beginning of the new beginnings. Always remember, God's process is worth the pain.

You may not fully understand it, but God is about to take you through a metamorphosis too. In fact, I am sure it's already started in your heart, whether you've noticed it or not. I'll explain more about this in the next chapter. Before I share the prophetic word and unpack it strategically and scripturally throughout this book, I need to offer some baseline definitions.

What Metamorphosis Really Means

When you hear the word "metamorphosis" you may hold an image in your mind of what it means. Taking the time to explore the actual definitions is insightful. The meaning of metamorphosis is richer than I thought and worth exploring so we can connect with the heart of the Father in the prophetic word I'll share later in this chapter.

According to the online dictionary *Merriam-Webster*, metamorphoses means, "a change of physical form, structure, or substance especially by supernatural means; the metamorphosis of humans into animals."

I found it absolutely fascinating that *Merriam-Webster* used the word "supernatural" to describe metamorphosis. Indeed, what the Lord is doing and will do in the lives of willing believers, churches and Kingdom companies this year is altogether supernatural. We could not possibly orchestrate the events that fuel our metamorphosis.

Indeed, many would not willfully choose to walk through the painful trials God allows to perfect our faith (see James 1:3). And we cannot change ourselves.

A secondary definition of metamorphosis is "a striking alteration in appearance, character, or circumstances." The metamorphosis that's underway will so radically change us—and institutions that give Jesus the preeminence—that some people won't recognize us. Saul experienced this type of metamorphosis.

The prophet Samuel prophesied, "The Spirit of the Lord will come upon you, and you will prophesy with them. And you will be turned into another man" (1 Samuel 10:6).

The third meaning of metamorphosis listed in this dictionary is "a typically marked and more or less abrupt developmental change in the form or structure of an animal (such as a butterfly or a frog) occurring subsequent to birth or hatching the metamorphosis of caterpillars into butterflies."

Many times before God can birth something new through you, he has to birth something new in you, such as the fruit of the Spirit, a persevering heart, or greater integrity.

Dictionary.com has a slightly different meaning of metamorphosis; one that sheds additional light on what many are already experiencing and what others should expect in the days and months ahead: "a profound change in form from one stage to the next in the life history of an organism, as from the caterpillar to the pupa and from the pupa to the adult butterfly; a complete change of form, structure, or substance, as transformation by magic or witchcraft; any complete change in appearance, character, circumstances, etc."

Prophecy: A Metamorphosis is Underway

I heard the Lord say, "A metamorphosis is underway. I will bring the change I've promised, first little by little and then an outward manifestation of an inner working I have been doing in My people. That metamorphosis will spill out from the spirits of My people into the spheres they influence in the seven mountains.

"Transformed business leaders will see their companies as ministry hubs. Transformed politicians will see their cities as congregations. Transformed cities will see mass salvations. I am calling those who have struggled in past seasons to make one more push because that last push will birth something in you and through you like the world has never seen and like nothing you could even imagine.

"I have allowed you to go through struggles—through suffering—so that I could use you as a compassionate change agent in the earth. You have authority. You have influence. You have power. You have an anointing. I intend to use you to comfort those who face disaster and to strengthen the weak. I intend to use you to lift others up, even those who dragged you down.

"You have been changed and are changing from glory to glory. The glory that rested upon you during the struggle is increasing as you step into the assignment I am giving you to see transformation all around you. You carry the kingdom. Releasing the kingdom into atmospheres around you and watch the darkness flee as the brilliance of My love works through you by faith. Have a confidence that I have called you, I have equipped you and I am sending you—and that I am with you always."

I see widespread metamorphosis. I see metamorphosis in people, in companies, in churches, and in societies. The metamorphosis is coming out of an intense struggle in the hearts and minds of people. It's even coming out of church splits and past moral failures in leadership. And it's coming from a changing of the guard in cities, states and nations. Many will come to realize the reality of Genesis 50:20 and Romans 8:28 in 2018 and in the years that follow.

Genesis 5:20 teaches this important principle: what the enemy meant for evil, God will work for good to save many. And Romans 8:28 promises us when we love Him and pray, He will work even the most horrific situations into something that benefits us and His purpose for our lives.

In the chapters ahead, we'll explore the concepts of metamorphosis as we dig through the prophecy so we can prepare our hearts to understand what God is doing and get into agreement with Him. Allow the Holy Spirit to challenge you as ready yourself for the season we're in. Pray this prayer with me:

Father, in the name of Jesus, I thank You that You love me too much to leave me the way I am. You have a metamorphosis in mind. Help me yield to the work You are doing in my mind, will and emotions. Help me not to resist the hand of the Potter. Shape me, make me, mold me into the image of your dear Son, for Your glory.

CHAPTER 2
WHAT THE BIBLE SAYS ABOUT METAMORPHOSIS

"Have a confidence that I have called you, I have equipped you and I am sending you—and that I am with you always."

Metamorphosis is a concept we find throughout the pages of the Bible. We watch God morph dust from the ground into the first man and Adam became a living creature (see Genesis 2:7). We know Adam committed high treason against the Most High God and disrupted our Creator's perfect will for mankind.

Thankfully, Jesus manifested in the form of a man and walked the earth as sinless man to pay the price for Adam's transgression—and ours.

A miraculous metamorphosis took place when we accepted Jesus as our Lord and Savior. We were translated out of the kingdom of darkness, where we were slaves to sin and servants to unrighteousness. We were translated into God's kingdom of light, where we are servants of God with newness of life (see Colossians 1:13).

Indeed, our first metamorphosis was the miracle of salvation. 2 Corinthians 5:17 tells us: "Therefore, if any man is in Christ, he is a new creature. Old things have passed away. Look, all things have become new."

God has a metamorphosis in mind for you that will strikingly alter countenance, your character and the negative circumstances that have plagued you. Call it radical breakthrough.

My first metamorphosis took place in a county jail, where I spent 40 days fighting for my future. I was falsely accused of a crime I did not commit at a time when I was all-out running from Jesus. I had hit rock bottom. I was facing five years in prison on bogus charges; and this after my husband abandoned me for a woman half his age. It looked like my two-year-old daughter was about to be orphaned.

But God in His great mercy had a different plan. When I surrendered my life to Jesus in the general population of a county jail, He began doing a fast work in my heart, in my mind and even in my physical body. In fact, I was 40 pounds overweight when I was arrested. During those 40 days in jail, I lost all 40 pounds. The day my vindication came—the day I was released from jail with all charges wiped away just like Jesus wiped away my sin at the new birth—there was not only a striking alteration in my character and circumstances, there was a striking alteration in my appearance.

In fact, I looked so different the corrections officers fingerprinted me before they would allow me to leave to make sure I was the same person.

The truth is, I was not the same person as I was when I walked in. I had undergone a spiritual, mental and physical metamorphosis. I have undergone many stages of metamorphosis since then, as we all do. Philippians 1:6 assures us, "He who began a good work in you will perfect it until the day of Jesus Christ." Our metamorphosis will not be complete until Jesus comes back and we are changed in a moment, in the twinkling of an eye (see 1 Corinthians 15:52). We will continue maturing in Him.

A Mind Metamorphosis

Metamorphosis begins in our hearts but must ultimately reach our minds in order to affect our will to walk in the change God has orchestrated in our lives. Paul spoke with the urgency of the Holy Spirit when he wrote these words to the church at Rome:

"I urge you therefore, brothers, by the mercies of God, that you present your bodies as a living sacrifice, holy, and acceptable to God, which is your reasonable service of worship. 2 Do not be conformed to this world, but be transformed by the renewing of your mind, that you may prove what is the good and acceptable and perfect will of God" (Romans 12:1-2).

I challenge you to meditate on the Amplified Classic version of these verses:

"I appeal to you therefore, brethren, and beg of you in view of [all] the mercies of God, to make a decisive dedication of your bodies [presenting all your members and faculties] as a living sacrifice, holy (devoted, consecrated) and well pleasing to God, which is your reasonable (rational, intelligent) service and spiritual worship.

"Do not be conformed to this world (this age), [fashioned after and adapted to its external, superficial customs], but be transformed (changed) by the [entire] renewal of your mind [by its new ideals and its new attitude], so that you may prove [for yourselves] what is the good and acceptable and perfect will of God, even the thing which is good and acceptable and perfect [in His sight for you]."

You can maximize this season of rapid metamorphosis by pressing into the admonition in Romans 12:1-2. Along these same lines, when you understand Proverbs 23:7 is unshakeable truth, this verse will fuel your spirit to submit to the apostle Paul's Spirit-inspired exhortation to the church at Rome. Proverbs 23:7 assures us we morph into what we think about. Consider some of the translations of this verse:

"For as he thinks within himself, so is he..." (NASB)

"For as he thinketh in his heart, so is he..." (KJV)

"For as he thinks in his soul, so is he" (Jubilee Bible 2000)

"For as he reckoneth within himself, so is he" (English Revised Version)

God wants to morph you into a new glory. The enemy is also working to morph you through your thought life. He uses vain imaginations that exalt themselves against the knowledge of God (see 2 Corinthians 10:5). The battle for who you will become—what you will morph into—truly is in the mind. In this season, we must be especially diligent to cast down vain imaginations and take Paul's instructions in Philippians 4:8 (AMPC):

"Whatever is true, whatever is worthy of reverence and is honorable and seemly, whatever is just, whatever is pure, whatever is lovely and lovable, whatever is kind and winsome and gracious, if there is any virtue and excellence, if there is anything worthy of praise, think on and weigh and take account of these things [fix your minds on them]."

Paul also offers a warning and a promise regarding our mindsets in Romans 8:5-6: "For those who live according to the flesh set their minds on the things of the flesh, but those who live according to the Spirit, the things of the Spirit. To be carnally minded is death, but to be spiritually minded is life and peace, for the carnal mind is hostile toward God, for it is not subject to the law of God, nor indeed can it be, and those who are in the flesh cannot please God."

A Faith Metamorphosis

God is working in us to root out doubt so He can move us to the next level of faith. (I talk more about overcoming doubt in my book, *Doubtless: Faith that Overcomes the World.*) Romans 1:17 speaks of moving from faith to faith.

The AMPC translation of this verse assures us the gospel reveals our righteousness in Christ that is "both springing from faith and leading to faith [disclosed through the way of faith that arouses to more faith. As it is written, the man who through faith is just and upright shall live by faith."

God wants us to live by faith, not by fear, not by doubt, and not by double-mindedness. James 1:8 (AMPC) speaks of this double-mindedness and its impact on your next level: "[For being as he is] a man of two minds (hesitating, dubious, irresolute), [he is] unstable and unreliable and uncertain about everything [he thinks, feels, decides]."

Many in this season will undergo a faith metamorphosis that will bring the stability they need to carry out His will in their lives. In past seasons where you've faltered, stumbled and fallen in the face of enemy attacks, this faith metamorphosis will refire your endurance and refuel steadfastness that rejects hesitancy. You're going to have newfound faith to go for it as you follow the command God gave Joshua! The Word says:

"This Book of the Law must not depart from your mouth. Meditate on it day and night so that you may act carefully according to all that is written in it. For then you will make your way successful, and you will be wise. Have not I commanded you? Be strong and courageous. Do not be afraid or dismayed, for the Lord your God is with you wherever you go" (Joshua 1:8-9).

God is morphing the weak faith of many to fervent faith through the gift of hunger. Where you see fervency, you see salvations. Where you see fervency, you see miracles. Where you see fervency, you see deliverance. Where you see fervency, you see the spirit of Christ showing up on the scene to work with those who believe.

Merriam-Webster defines the word "fervent" as very hot or glowing. When something is fervent, it is "exhibiting or marked by a great intensity or feeling." Let's drill down a little deeper to the roots of the word. The English word "fervency" comes from the Greek word "zeo." It literally means "to boil."

Can you imagine? Have you ever watched water boil? It bubbles up with utter intensity—and sometimes it even escapes the confines of the pot. Boiling water can't hide its expression. In fact, if you come too close to a pot of boiling water, the steam alone will get your attention.

Noteworthy is the fact that boiling is a way to purify water. As we are boiling over for God, I believe our souls are being purified. Think about it for a minute. We won't be consumed with demonic imaginations when we are consumed with a godly focus. There is no devilish playground in the fervent spirit. A fervent spirit is on fire for God. A fervent spirit is a passionate spirit. A fervent spirit is a zealous spirit. God likes fervency. (I write more about this in my book, *Fervent Faith*.)

How do you cooperate with the grace of God to turn weak faith—or even lukewarm faith—into fervent faith? First, understand that faith is a substance that grows in your heart as you hear the Word of God.

Hebrews 11 explains, "Now faith is the substance of things hoped for, the evidence of things not seen." The Message translation puts it this way: "It's our handle on what we can't see." The NLT shares: "Faith is the confidence that what we hope for will actually happen." And we know faith comes by hearing and hearing by the Word of God (see Romans 10:17).

As the prophetic word says, "Have a confidence that I have called you, I have equipped you and I am sending you—and that I am with you always."

You build faith, which is confidence in God's Word, by reading, confessing and meditating on the Word. Pray this prayer with me: *Father, in the name of Jesus, I come to You with a humble heart asking You to help me renew my mind. Help me take into captivity every thought that opposes Your will for my life. Give me a hunger for Your Word that exceeds my hunger for natural food. Empower me by Your Spirit to press into what you are doing in my life in this season of metamorphosis, in Jesus' name. Amen.*

CHAPTER 3
FROM GLORY TO GLORY

"You have been changed and are changing from glory to glory."

That faith metamorphosis we discussed in that last chapter will lead to a glory metamorphosis as Paul wrote in 2 Corinthians 3:18-19:

"And all of us, as with unveiled face, [because we] continued to behold [in the Word of God] as in a mirror the glory of the Lord, are constantly being transfigured into His very own image in ever increasing splendor and from one degree of glory to another; [for this comes] from the Lord [Who is] the Spirit." Jesus Himself made this audacious statement in John 17:22 (AMPC): "I have given to them the glory and honor which You have given Me..."

What did Paul actually mean? What was Jesus really saying? One has to turn to the Greek to fully understand by what they meant by glory. The Greek word for glory in these verses is "doxa."

According to *The KJV New Testament Greek Lexicon*, it means: "splendor, brightness, magnificence, dignity, grace, the kingly majesty of the Messiah, and the glorious condition of blessedness into which is appointed and promised that true Christians shall enter after their Savior's return from heaven."

There are levels of glory, and God morphs or shifts us from one level to another. With greater glory comes greater freedom. Christ in us is the hope of ultimate glory (see Colossians 3:37). But while we walk in these earthly bodies, we can morph into new glories as we gaze upon His beauty. God has called us to His own glory (see 2 Peter 1:3). In reality, we are reflecting HIs glory at work in us. His glory first transforms us, then radiates through us to transform the world around us.

The Lord spoke these words to my heart:

"My glory is not to be taken lightly. My glory is not to be mocked. My glory is to be entered into with reverence, with holy fear and trembling, with awe... For I am indeed pouring out My glory more and more as the darkness begins to rise in the earth.

"I am determined that My people not only taste and see My glory, but walk in My glory to demonstrate to a lost world that I am a living God and a loving God. I am looking for carriers of My glory who will steward My presence and release My gifts without seeking their own glory.

"I am looking for those who will host My presence with kingdom understanding and look beyond a single meeting to the transformative power of My Spirit in the earth. I am calling on you now to press into My glory, not for your sake but for the sake of the nations. My glory will indeed cover the earth like the waters cover the sea."

CHAPTER 4
WHAT CHANGES HAS GOD PROMISED YOU?

"I am calling those who have struggled in past seasons to make one more push because that last push will birth something in you and through you like the world has never seen and like nothing you could even imagine."

Remember how excited you were when you got that prophetic word five, 10 or even 15 years ago? You set your heart to prepare yourself to walk it out. You confessed it out of your mouth. You declared it shall come to pass. You prayed it through.

You did everything you were supposed to do, but that prophetic word still hasn't come to pass. In fact, it may even look like the exact opposite is happening in your life. It may look like to enemy has already robbed your prophecy. It may seem like the prophetic word will never come to pass.

Recently, the Lord showed me in a *Mornings With the Holy Spirit* prayer broadcast, which I do Mondays through Fridays on my Facebook and Periscope—that the reason so many people are feeling rumblings, seeing strategic persecution and otherwise experiencing an increase in warfare is because some of the prayers you've prayed and some of the prophetic words you received many years ago are about to come to pass.

See, God has to work a metamorphosis in you before He can answer those some of those prayers and manifest some of those prophetic words. You have to walk through some things, change your mind about some things, open your heart to new people and close the door to old relationships that were holding you back. All of this is part of your metamorphosis. If God is cutting things away even now, rejoice and know that He's about to add much more back.

Now is your moment of decision. Will you give up on that tried-and-tested prophetic words you know that you know that you know are from God? Or will you go back to the author of that prophecy—Jesus—and remind Him of the prophetic words?

Jacob's Vow at Bethel

Jacob got a prophetic word from God while he was fleeing his angry brother, Esau, whom he cheated out of his birthright. Imagine the scene: Jacob was traveling alone from Beersheba toward Haran, and when the sun started setting, he decided to rest. He used a rock for a pillow and had prophetic dreams of "a ladder that was set up on the earth, and its top reached to heaven; and there the angels of God were ascending and descending on it" (Gen. 28:12). Next came a prophecy that was exceedingly abundantly above all he could ask or think:

"I am the Lord God of Abraham your father and the God of Isaac; the land on which you lie I will give to you and your descendants. Also your descendants shall be as the dust of the earth; you shall spread abroad to the west and the east, to the north and the south; and in you and in your seed all the families of the earth shall be blessed. Behold, I am with you and will keep you wherever you go, and will bring you back to this land; for I will not leave you until I have done what I have spoken to you" (vv. 13-15).

Jacob believed the prophetic word, set up a pillar to God, poured oil upon it and made a vow to give a tenth to God if He kept him safe during his journey, gave him food and clothing, and allowed him to reach his father's house in peace.

Of course, God kept up His part of the covenant. Despite being cheated by his uncle Laban for more than a decade, Jacob prospered wildly in every respect in Haran. He had exceeding abundant children, livestock and favor with God.

Wrestling With God

Finally fed up with Laban's dishonesty, Jacob decided to return to his country. Laban pursued him, and Jacob boldly confronted his uncle—but when Jacob learned that Esau was coming out to meet him, fear struck his heart. Jacob did what we need to do when it looks like our prophetic word can't possibly come to pass—when it looks like the devil is devouring our prophetic dreams. When the enemy comes in with fear that what God said will never happen, we need to take the prophetic word back to its author in prayer.

"Then Jacob said, 'O God of my father Abraham and God of my father Isaac, the Lord who said to me, "Return to your country and to your family, and I will deal well with you": I am not worthy of the least of all the mercies and of all the truth which You have shown Your servant; for I crossed over this Jordan with my staff, and now I have become two companies.

Deliver me, I pray, from the hand of my brother, from the hand of Esau; for I fear him, lest he come and attack me and the mother with the children. For You said, "I will surely treat you well, and make your descendants as the sand of the sea, which cannot be numbered for multitude"'" (Gen. 32:9-12).

But Jacob didn't stop there. Jacob wrestled with God over the issue until the break of day. You'll recall the determined words of Jacob's mouth: "I will not let You go until You bless me!" (v. 26). Jacob got his blessing, but he walked away with a limp.

Of course, God always intended to keep his prophetic word to Jacob. There was never a question in God's mind that He would watch over His word to perform it (Jer. 1:12). And the same holds true for you. Although some prophecies are conditional, some are set in stone—no man on earth or devil in hell can stop what God has planned. But we can stop it with our doubt, unbelief, fearful mindset, complacency and apathy.

So if you've been waiting for months, years or decades for a prophecy to come to pass—and when you're afraid people and circumstances are going to kill your promise—do what Jacob did. Pray. Remind God of His prophetic word. Wrestle with God in prayer until you have the faith to get up and run toward His perfect will despite what things look like—even if you have to run with a limp.

Pray this prayer with me: *Father, in the name of Jesus I come boldly to Your throne of grace. I put You in remembrance of the promises You released over my life. I ask You for the grace to fight the good fight of faith for Your perfect will in my life. Give me the endurance to wage war with accurate prophecies for Your glory. Help me not to grow weary in well doing so I can reap the harvest of prayer answers and prophetic promises You have in Your heart for me.*

CHAPTER 5
WHAT MOUNTAIN ARE
YOU CALLED TO?

"That metamorphosis will spill out from the spirits of My people into the spheres they influence in the seven mountains. Transformed business leaders will see their companies as ministry hubs. Transformed politicians will see their cities as congregations. Transformed cities will see mass salvations."

Loren Cunningham, founder of Youth With a Mission, and the late Bill Bright, founder of Campus Crusade for Christ (now called CRU), received the same revelation from the Lord in 1975:

In order to revolutionize the world for Jesus, the church needs to wield influence in the seven mountains of society—religion, family, education, government, media, arts and entertainment, and business.

God gave mankind dominion over the earth in Genesis 1:26: "Then God said, 'Let us make man in our image, after our likeness, and let them have dominion over the fish of the sea, and over the birds of the air, and over the livestock, and over all the earth, and over every creeping thing that creeps on the earth.'"

Of course, we know Adam committed high treason. Later Jesus took dominion back from the devil and gave His followers a mandate to rule and reign with Him (see 2 Timothy 2:12). We will rule and reign in greater measure in eternity but there is a rulership in this age. Jesus said, "Occupy until I come" (Luke 19:13). That Greek word occupy is "pragmateuomai." *The KJV New Testament Greek Lexicon* translates it as: "to be occupied in anything; to carry on a business."

As Jesus was about His Father's business, we must be occupied with our Father's business in the sphere of influence to which He has called us (see Luke 4:29). We are charged with walking worthy of the vocation to which we are called (see Ephesians 4:1). As ministers of reconciliation and ambassadors of Christ (see 2 Corinthians 5:18-20), we may have a natural occupation but we also have a spiritual vocation. And we are warned not to hide our light under a bushel (see Matthew 5:15).

Entire books have been written on the seven mountains of society. Beyond Bright and Cunningham, men of God like Francis Schaeffer, Bob Buford, Os Hillman, Ed Silvoso and Lance Wallnau have worked to forward this revelation. We don't have time in this short book to explore all the facets of this theology, but we will look briefly at each of the seven mountains.

Every believer has been given a sphere of influence and authority in one of these mountains. Exploring each mountain individually will help you clearly identify, with the leading of the Holy Spirit, the mountain to which you are called. The following definitions are attributed to Generals International's Reformation Prayer Network, whose primary goal is to be a catalyst through prayer and righteous activism to bring change to these areas of societal influence. You can find more about the network at www.generals.org/rpn. You can also join my prayer movement at www.awakeningblaze.com.

The Mountain of Religion

Every society has some type of belief in a superior being or beings. In the east, religions tend to be polytheistic (many gods) or outright idolatrous (such as Hinduism and Buddhism). Although these religions are thousands of years old, they nonetheless continue to thrive today.

In the west, Christianity and Catholicism are predominant, but postmodern views are increasingly being accepted and the concept of God is being rejected. This is especially true in Europe.

The Christian Church is described in the Greek language as the ecclesia. Literally translated, the word ecclesia means "governing body." Although we don't condone theocracies, this translation suggests that the Church should have great influence in all other spheres that make up a society. With a plethora of categorized religions around the world, it's the Church's responsibility to reach the lost with the love and Gospel of Jesus Christ, and expand the Kingdom in ministerial efforts, both nationally and internationally.

The Mountain of Family

In any functional society, the family is the "building block" of the community. Throughout the Bible, you will find familial examples that portray how we ought to live our lives today. God desires that men, women, and children within a family be united as one in His love. After all, He is the ultimate Father (Romans 8:14-17).

The families of the United States have been under constant and prolonged attack. Today, the assailants are fatherlessness, divorce (50% rate in secular and Christian marriages), abuse, homosexual marriage, pornography, and other negative influences have brought great dysfunction to American life. God is calling fathers and mothers (both spiritual and biological) to bring order to the chaos that the enemy has unleashed against families in America. He also wants to bring healing to marriages and relationships within families in order to maintain a moral foundation for children in the future to stand upon.

The Mountain of Education

At one time the education system of America unapologetically incorporated the Bible, prayer to the God of the Bible, and biblical values in every aspect of school life. Not coincidentally, this system produced a people that produced the most powerful and prosperous nation the earth has ever seen.

Now, the children of our nation are inundated with liberal ideologies, atheistic teaching and postmodern principles in our public schools and in most universities (including many Christian institutions).

Put simply; they are being indoctrinated with often false, biased and anti-biblical information. A re-introduction of biblical truth and Bible-centric values is the key to renewal and restoration in America's failing educational system.

The Mountain of Government

Proverbs 14:34 states that, "righteousness exalts a nation, but sin is a reproach to any people." Many times, as exemplified in the Old Testament, a nation's moral standards are dependent on those exhibited by its leaders (or predominant political party). While each individual is responsible for his or her own sins; the fact remains that people are greatly influenced by those moral (or lack thereof) that popular leaders adopt.

The progressive liberal agenda, empowered by well-known men and women in the arts and entertainment industries, have made significant gains in the political arena over the past few decades. In fact, many liberal groups, such as the ACLU, seek to remove anything related to God or Christianity from the governmental and educational systems because of a misapplied interpretation of the phrase,

"separation of church and state." We must see a shift in this arena in order to preserve the Christian heritage that America was founded upon. The goal is to put in place righteous political leaders that will positively affect all aspects of government.

The Mountain of Media

The media mountain includes news sources such as radio, TV news stations, newspapers, Internet news and opinion (blog) sites and etc. The media has the potential to sway popular opinion on current issues based upon its reporting, which is not always truthful or accurate. In the 2008 elections, the liberal "elite" media played a vital role, especially in the Presidential race. Their generally supportive and positive reporting greatly influenced the outcome.

There has been a rise in Christian news services, which is needed. However, to bring transformation to the mountain of media, Christians who are gifted for and called into this type of work must be willing to report righteously and truthfully in the secular marketplace.

The Mountain of Arts & Entertainment

In this mountain we find some of the most influential forces shaping our society. Music, filmmaking, television, social media, and the performing arts drive the cultural tastes, values and standards of a nation's citizens, particularly its youth.

With a heavy reliance on the strong appeal of sex, drugs and alcohol, the arts and entertainment industries wield significant influence. The body of Christ needs powerful, righteous men and women who are not afraid to take their God-given talent into the arts and entertainment arenas.

People ready to further His purposes, while impacting those who are lost in darkness and would not otherwise be interested in any kind of Christian message in traditional forms.

The Mountain of Business
The ability to literally create wealth through ingenuity, enterprise, creativity and effort and is a God-given gift and a universal impulse. The markets and economic systems that emerge whenever people are free to pursue buying and selling become the lifeblood of a nation. This includes anything from farms to small businesses to large corporations.

Of course, this realm is prone to corruption through idolatry, greed and covetousness.

In response, the Church must embrace its responsibility to train up those who are called into the marketplace to manage businesses and provide leadership with integrity and honesty. We believe it is the Lord's will to make his people prosperous and that He desires for His Church to use its wealth to finance the work of Kingdom expansion. Simply put: Prosperity with a purpose.

Millennials Hold a Key
Although every believer is called to influence their sphere, Cunningham sees the Millennial generation as ripe for impact in this hour. In an interview with Hillman, Cunningham said:

___

"One, they are more concerned about the poor and needy than any nation that we've seen in a long time in the generations. They're also global in their thinking, and they don't think of just their own nation. And because of this, and their connectivity because of the media through IT, through the various forms of the Internet and so on, they are really connected around the world.

"Now when they are sparked by God, and see that God has the answers through them, to change the nations, and find out, 'Hey, we can do it in the category God's already given us a gifting and a calling to,' so it all comes back to their gifts and callings. The gifts and callings of God are without repentance. And so, if they're called into business, or called into education or called into missions and the church or whatever the category is, they can see God coming in and make a change, because we don't have to use old paradigms, we can use the new. And this generation is going to find them, because the greatest form of communication is on us, through the Internet. There's never been a time like this."

Pray this prayer with me: *Father, in the name of Jesus, help me to identify the mountain I am to conquer for Your glory. Like Caleb and Joshua as they spied out the Promised Land, help me see myself as well able to take the land. Give me a "different spirit" as they had so I will charge ahead in your grace to accomplish Your will in the mountain of influence in which you've called me to operate."*

CHAPTER 6
A REASON FOR THE STRUGGLE

*"I have allowed you to go through struggles—
through suffering—so that I could use you as a
compassionate change agent in the earth."*

By definition, struggling implies great effort—
even violent efforts—in the middle of a difficult
circumstance. Struggling brings with it suffering.
We see this struggle and suffering played out in
the butterfly's metamorphosis.

A butterfly lays an egg that hatches a
caterpillar. As these creatures grow, scientists say
caterpillars shed their skin four or five times. By
the time the caterpillar is fully grown it can be up
to 100 times larger than it was at birth—but that's
just the beginning.

The caterpillar is ready for the next stage
of its metamorphosis known as a pupa. In this life
stage, the creature is being transformed little by
little until it is formed into an entirely new being;
into a mature form.

Scientists say there is little movement when the caterpillar is in this pupa or "chrysalis" phase. It may look like nothing is happening, but great change is taking place as legs, wings, eyes and other parts of the butterfly are forming. But a sort of hard shell forms around the pupa to guard it against predators who would take advantage of its vulnerable state.

After a period of time, the pupa breaks open and a butterfly emerges. The butterfly struggles to break through completely. Scientists say if anyone helps the butterfly at this point, the morphed creature will not be able to spread its wings and fly. The struggle to emerge strengthens its wings.

Spiritual Parallels in the Butterfly's Struggle

There are so many spiritual parallels in the struggle from caterpillar to butterfly. As a young Christian, you grow, grow, grow but at some point after you are stable in Christ God seeks to mature you in a deeper way. He has a metamorphosis in mind. We enter into a process—not just once in our lives but at various stages in our walk with God—where Christ is formed more fully in us (see Galatians 4:19) and we grow more into His stature (see Ephesians 4:13).

During this transition—this Spirit-inspired metamorphosis—the change is slower than we'd like. Sometimes it begins before we understand fully what is happening and sometimes it doesn't end when we'd like it to. Most times we feel fear during the transition. There seems to be little forward movement; little progress in our lives. We don't see anything happening.

During a metamorphosis, we must remember to walk by faith and not by sight (see 2 Corinthians 5:7). We must refuse to live by how we feel or even what we hear but what we know—what the Bible says about us and what Scripture promises us.

We must believe He who began a good work in us when we became new creatures in Christ will perfect us little by little (see Philippians 1:6). We may feel like we're holding on for dear life and we may be. But we must hold on because newness of life awaits.

The good news is during times of metamorphosis—mass transition—God is protecting us. Yes, the enemy comes and tries to trick us into abandon the process. Yes, the enemy works to convince us to abort the purpose and plans of God for our lives.

In the right time—in the kairos moment—we come to the edge of breakthrough. Often times, the struggle is the greatest in the moments just before the breakthrough occurs.

We see this illustrated in the natural birthing process. The woman often feels like she cannot push one more time, but she finds the strength to continue laboring for the newness of life that has long been hidden and is now finding its birth.

During the struggle, we may look to our friends to help but often God won't let them help us. He alone wants to serve as our Helper. He uses this struggle to strengthen our spirits so we can soar with Him when we emerge with a new beauty, grace, power and anointing.

The words of Thomas Paine, an English-born American political activist, philosopher, political theorist, and revolutionary from the 1800s, always strike my spirit.

He said, "The harder the conflict, the more glorious the triumph." Those words right true. After you undergo the pain, the suffering, the struggle and the surrender of a metamorphosis by faith you will realize a new level of glory.

Changing Our Perspective on Suffering

Job went through radical suffering. He lost his sheep, his oxen, his camels—which represent finances and provision in modern times. He lost his servants and every single one of his sons and daughters. Finally, he lost his health—and he almost lost his mind. During a metamorphosis, the enemy brings suffering in four primary areas: our mind, our relationships, our finances and our bodies.

The definition of suffering is interesting. It means "to be forced to endure." When suffering comes your way, you are forced to endure it. What is the alternative? What choice do you have? When you are suffering, it feels like the entire world crashing in around you. It feels like you are helpless, there is no way of escape and nothing is ever going to change. When you are suffering it often feels like people are letting you down; that God is letting you down. And we know the devil always kicks you when you are down.

The good news is you can choose how you suffer. You can receive God's grace by asking Him to help you see things the way He sees them or you can stay frustrated and miserable. I'm reminded of a time when Paul was suffering. We read the account in 2 Corinthians 12:8-10:

"And lest I should be exalted above measure by the abundance of revelations, a thorn was given me in the flesh, a messenger of Satan, to torment me, lest I be exalted above measure. I asked the Lord three times that this thing might depart from me. But He said to me, 'My grace is sufficient for you, for My strength is made perfect in weakness.' Therefore most gladly I will boast in my weaknesses, that the power of Christ may rest upon me. So I take pleasure in weaknesses, in reproaches, in hardships, in persecutions, and in distresses for Christ's sake. For when I am weak, then I am strong."

When you are struggling in the metamorphosis, when you are suffering in the transition, lean into Him. He will help you break through to the other side as you wait upon Him, and you'll rise up with wings as eagles with a prophetic perspective you didn't have before. Let these truths change your perspective on the suffering so you can move from a victim to a victor mentality.

Rejoice Radically

We must learn to be radical rejoicers in any and every situation. Paul told us in Romans 5:3-5 (ESV), "More than that, we rejoice in our sufferings, knowing that suffering produces endurance, and endurance produces character, and character produces hope, and hope does not put us to shame, because God's love has been poured into our hearts through the Holy Spirit who has been given to us."

James 1:2-4 (ESV) admonishes us to, "Count it all joy, my brothers, when you meet trials of various kinds, for you know that the testing of your faith produces steadfastness. And let steadfastness have its full effect, that you may be perfect and complete, lacking in nothing."

Those are the Scriptures we don't like to read when we're suffering. But we can and should rejoice knowing you are being morphed into the image of Christ.

And 1 Peter 1:6-7 (ESV) offers these encouraging words: "In this you rejoice, though now for a little while, if necessary, you have been grieved by various trials, so that the tested genuineness of your faith—more precious than gold that perishes though it is tested by fire—may be found to result in praise and glory and honor at the revelation of Jesus Christ."

Develop Radical Trust

I know it feels like you are fighting alone at the height of your metamorphosis. Believe me, I know. Still, nobody can possibly understand what it's like to walk in your shoes. Many in the Bible felt like they were fighting alone. Elijah felt like he was fighting alone. So did Samson. Paul was often deserted in his travels. But you're never really fighting alone because the Lord is for you.

Jesus understands your suffering. Hebrews 4:15 (ESV) tells us, " For we do not have a high priest who is unable to sympathize with our weaknesses, but one who in every respect has been tempted as we are, yet without sin." And Isaiah 43:2 (ESV) assures us, "When you pass through the waters, I will be with you; and through the rivers, they shall not overwhelm you; when you walk through fire you shall not be burned, and the flame shall not consume you."

God will release you into your new season—out of that pupa—at the perfect time. Often times we look for a way of escape but we must only take God's way of escape. 1 Corinthians 10:13 tells us, "No temptation has overtaken you that is not common to man. God is faithful, and he will not let you be tempted beyond your ability, but with the temptation he will also provide the way of escape, that you may be able to endure it."

Psalm 34:19 (ESV) declares, "Many are the afflictions of the righteous, but the Lord delivers him out of them all." And Psalm 22:24 (ESV) tells us, "For he has not despised or abhorred the affliction of the afflicted, and he has not hidden his face from him, but has heard, when he cried to him." The timing of God's deliverance is perfect. His arm is not too short that He can't reach down and deliver.

Keep Eternal Glory in Mind

We need to keep an eternal mindset in the midst of suffering. Our radical suffering will lead to radical glory. Consider these Scriptures, which will help you keep your mind set on things above and not merely on the things of this earth during your metamorphosis (see Colossians 3:2).

"For this light momentary affliction is preparing for us an eternal weight of glory beyond all comparison…" (2 Corinthians 4:17, ESV).

50

"For I consider that the sufferings of this present time are not worth comparing with the glory that is to be revealed to us" (Romans 8:18, ESV).

"Blessed is the man who remains steadfast under trial, for when he has stood the test he will receive the crown of life, which God has promised to those who love him" (James 1:12, ESV).

"And if children, then heirs—heirs of God and fellow heirs with Christ, provided we suffer with him in order that we may also be glorified with him" (Romans 8:17, ESV).

"He will wipe away every tear from their eyes, and death shall be no more, neither shall there be mourning, nor crying, nor pain anymore, for the former things have passed away" (Revelation 21:4, ESV).

What We Can Learn From the Teacup

Joyce Meyer once told a story that has gone somewhat viral on the Internet. Still, you may not have read it. Let this inspire you in the year of metamorphosis.

A couple went into an antique shop and saw this beautiful, beautiful magnificent little tea cup sitting high up on a shelf. And they just fell in love with that tea cup. They said, "We have got to have that teacup!" They were admiring the teacup—all of a sudden the teacup began to talk to them.

It said, "You know, I have not been always like this! There was a time when nobody would have wanted me. There was a time when I was not attractive at all. You see there was a time in my life when I was just an old, hard, gray lump of clay. And the master potter came along and he picked me up one day and he began to pat me and reshape me; and I said, "Stop it! What are you doing? That hurts! Ahhh... leave me alone!"" And he simply looked at me and said, "Not yet!"

And then he put me on this wheel and he began to spin me around, and around and around! And I got so dizzy and could hardly see where I was going anymore! I was losing it! Everything was spinning around and around and I felt sick to my stomach. And I said; "Let me off here!" and he said, "Not yet!"

Finally, the day came when I had taken on another shape. All of that spinning around finally gave me another shape. All of that patting and molding and squeezing and pinching gave me another shape. And all of a sudden he put me into this furnace! It is called the first firing. And 'twas so hot in there! Oh, I could not believe how hot it was. I thought, "I can't stand this! I'm going to die in here! 'Get me out of here'!!! Don't you love me?? (Crying.) Why are you leaving me in here?' You see, the oven door had glass in it and the master would just look in his eyes and he would not let me out!! But he would just smile at me and say, 'Not yet!'

Finally, the oven door opened and he took me out, set me on a shelf and I thought, "Whew! Thank God that is over!" Then he began to paint me all over with this stinky paint! Changing my color from gray to this pretty blue that I am now! And I said: 'This stuff stinks! It is choking me! (coughing) I don't like this smell! Stop it! Stop it! Stop it! Stop it! He would just say: "Not yet!"

Then he put me back in a second oven. It is called the second firing, and 'twas twice as hot as the first oven! And I thought, 'Now, I will die in here for sure! This is the end of me. This will finish me off! Get me out of here! I can't stand it! I can't stand it! Really, I am telling you I can't stand it! This is going to kill me! Get me out of here!" And he would just look through that glass and say: "Not yet!"

Then one day the door finally opened. He took me out and he put me up here on this shelf to let me cool off. After I cooled off, one day he came by and he handed me this mirror and I looked at myself and I could not believe how beautiful I was! I could not believe how I have changed! Why, I did not look anything at all like that old gray clay that I started out to be!

Now, I am this beautiful, little, delicate teacup! And everybody wants me now! But there was a time in my life when nobody wanted, nobody liked me, nobody paid any attention to me! They just kicked me around, walked on me.

But now I am special! But I wasn't always this way!

Pray this prayer with me: *Father, I know I am not where I need to be, but I thank You that I am not where I used to be. I'm grateful when I walk through the fire and through the waters, You are with me. You will never leave me or forsake me, even to the end of the age. Please give me the grace to endure this radical suffering and help me endure the pain of change on the way to the next glory, in Jesus' name.*

CHAPTER 7
PAYBACK FOR THE SUFFERING

"I intend to use you to comfort those who face disaster and to strengthen the weak. I intend to use you to lift others up, even those who dragged you down."

God is your vindicator, and He is readying you to receive restoration in your finances, relationships, health—or any other area the enemy has meddled. Keep in mind as you read these words God is a God of payback. He tells us, "Vengeance is mine, I will repay (Romans 12:19). He gave Job double for his trouble (see Job 42:10). He assures us the thief who is caught must repay seven times (see Proverbs 6:31). How do you ready yourself for payback?

Take Responsibility and Repent for Your Part

"I am responsible." Those are the first three words you need to say when adversity hits your life. No, I'm not saying you are responsible for all adversity that comes your way. But you are responsible for how you respond to it.

On the other hand, we do sometimes make poor decisions and open the door for the enemy to meddle in our minds. When adversity strikes, the first thing I do is examine my heart. Am I out of God's will? Did I open a door to the enemy somehow? Before we start chasing devils we need to chase God for a revelation of where the trouble lies.

Many are tempted to blame shift when things go wrong—pointing fingers at others for their own mistakes, failures and warfare. This is not a helpful perspective if you want to see things shift because blame is the guard for change. When you refuse to take responsibility for your part, you hinder your spiritual growth and your natural breakthrough.

Consider the words of the Preacher in Proverbs 28:13: "Whoever conceals his transgressions will not prosper, but he who confesses and forsakes them will obtain mercy." We see blame shifting at its best in Genesis 3:12-13 when God confronted Adam and Eve about disobeying His command and eating from the tree of the knowledge of good and evil.

"The man said, 'The woman whom you gave to be with me, she gave me fruit of the tree, and I ate.' Then the Lord God said to the woman, "What is this that you have done?" The woman said, 'The serpent deceived me, and I ate.'"

The blame game got them nowhere—they were expelled from the Garden of Eden. We need to be willing to repent—to change the way we think—if we want to see maximum payback in our lives.

Reject Guilt and Condemnation; Forgive Yourself

Some years ago, I lost nearly $100,000 cash in a bad real estate investment deal. I didn't have a word of the Lord to do it—but it seemed like God. Our pastor was pressuring everyone in the church to invest in real estate—to flip houses. He had a wrong motive and I missed God!

I beat myself up about that for years. The devil told me I was a poor steward. The devil plagued me with thoughts of how I could have used that money to pay for my daughter's college or sow into missions. The devil bombarded me with guilt and condemnation.

Thank God there is no condemnation in Christ (see Rom. 8:1). After I repented for missing God's warnings about the real estate investment, I received His forgiveness and shunned guilt and condemnation for good. I learned from the mistake. In the end, I got triple for my trial as I received an inheritance worth three times what I lost from a couple in the ministry who God led to sow valuable property into my life.

Let God Off the Hook

Many times we blame God—but God is not the robber—God is the vindicator. John 10:10 makes this absolutely clear: "The thief does not come, except to steal and kill and destroy. I came that they may have life, and that they may have it more abundantly."

God isn't destroying our dreams, stealing our money, sending our kids into sin, or putting sickness on our bodies. Why do bad things happen to good people? Because the devil is a bad devil. But God is a good God.

When Job was going through his trial, he lost everything. He lost his family, his livestock, his barns, his health—he lost it all. His wife said, "Curse God and die." He refused to blame God. He didn't put God on the hook and everything he lost at the enemy's hand was restored two-fold.

Forgive Those Who Robbed You

Forgiveness is not a feeling. It's not justifying what someone did. It's not even necessarily reconciling. Forgiveness is an act of your will. When you choose to forgive, your emotions will eventually line up with your will.

Keep in mind, your prayers for payback will not work if you don't forgive. Jesus puts it plainly in Mark 11:25: "And when you stand praying, forgive if you have anything against anyone, so that your Father who is in heaven may also forgive you your sins."

You can pray for pay back all day, but if you have unforgiveness in your heart, it hinders your petitions because you are in disobedience. You are not in God's will when you harbor unforgiveness. You can't receive payback from God when you are looking for payback from man.

Pray for Those Who Despitefully Used You

In Matthew 5:44-45, Jesus said: "But I say to you, love your enemies, bless those who curse you, do good to those who hate you, and pray for those who spitefully use you and persecute you, 45 that you may be sons of your Father who is in heaven. For He makes His sun rise on the evil and on the good and sends rain on the just and on the unjust."

Don't pray the, "Get 'em, God" prayer. Don't pray that He would convict them or make them feel bad. Pray the blessings you would pray for your closest friend or those who wronged you. Pray radical increase, favor, and peace over their lives. When you do this, many times the Holy Spirit will actually bless them with the conviction of their wrong.

Job endured a season of suffering, but then he saw radical restoration. The Bible tells us when he prayed for his friends who had persecuted him, the Lord restored double all he lost (see Job 42:10).

Bless Those Who Have Cursed You

"Bless" quite literally means to say good things about someone. Curse, by contrast, means to say evil things about someone. When people curse us, our flesh likes to curse them back. When people hurt us, we want to hurt them back. We want to tell everyone what they did and make them look bad. Move in the opposite spirit. Say good things about those who wrong you. That opens the door for payback.

Ask the Lord for Justice

After you've forgiven and blessed, you are ready to ask the Lord for Justice. The parable of the widow and the unjust judge is our model. Luke 18:1-6 reads:

"He told them a parable to illustrate that it is necessary always to pray and not lose heart. He said: 'In a city there was a judge who did not fear God or regard man. And a widow was in that city. She came to him, saying, 'Avenge me against my adversary.' He would not for a while. Yet afterward he said to himself, 'Though I do not fear God or respect man, yet because this widow troubles me, I will avenge her, lest by her continual coming she will weary me.'

"And the Lord said, 'Hear what the unjust judge says. And shall not God avenge His own elect and be patient with them, who cry day and night to Him? I tell you, He will avenge them speedily. Nevertheless, when the Son of Man comes, will He find faith on the earth?"

You can pray this prayer with me: Father, in the name of Jesus, I ask you to forgive those who hurt me, used me, robbed from me, and caused me pain. I forgive them and release them, and bless them, in the name of Jesus. I know I'm not wrestling against flesh and blood. Thank You, Lord, that You are a just God. Life may not be fair, but You are just. I ask You now to avenge me of my spiritual adversaries. Bring your justice swiftly. Bring back what the enemy stole, in the name of Your Son Jesus. Amen.

Pray this prayer with me: *Father, I forgive those who wronged me, maligned me, hurt me, wounded me, betrayed me or otherwise harmed me. I'm so grateful You are a God of restoration. Help me to avoid the temptation to take matters into my own hands; to see my own payback. Help me to wait upon Your timing for the vindication and restoration. Give me grace to walk in love with my enemies, in Jesus' name.*

CHAPTER 8
SHIFTING SPIRITUAL ATMOSPHERES

"You carry the kingdom. Releasing the kingdom into atmospheres around you and watch the darkness flee as the brilliance My love works through you by faith."

Before we can shift spiritual atmospheres around us, we have to shift our own personal spiritual atmosphere.

We all know what a season is, but we don't always know what season we're in. Spiritually speaking, a season is a period of time—that can be specific or indefinite.

We know that to everything there is a season, and a time for every purpose under heaven (see Ecclesiastes 3:1).

We know that we're not supposed to grow weary in well doing because we'll reap if we don't give up—in due season (see Galatians 6:9).

We know that if we meditate on the Word day and night we will stand like trees planted by the rivers of water, bringing forth fruit in its season and prospering in whatever we do (see Psalms 1:2-3).

But we must also know that it is God who changes the times and seasons (see Daniel 2:21). We can't change our own season, but we can position ourselves for a season shift.

Merriam-Webster describes a "shift" as to exchange for or replace by another; to change the place, position or direction of; to change gears; to go through a change." When the Holy Spirit said, "shifting season," it's easy to discern that He means changes are ahead. Some of you are going to shift from a time of sowing to a time of reaping. Others will shift from weeping to laughing. Still others will shift from lack to prosperity.

I'm reminded of the what God told Jeremiah, "For I know the plans that I have for you, says the Lord, plans for peace and not for evil, to give you a future and a hope" (Jeremiah 29:11). God has good plans for us in 2016. He wants to shift us out of what has held us back from His best and into His good, perfect and acceptable will (see Romans 12:2).

Creating a Climate for the Shift

Our part is to position ourselves for the shift—and that means creating a climate that sets the stage for God to move in our lives. Scientists will tell you that the earth's seasons have shifted in recent years—and they point to climate change as the foundation for the shift.

If we translate this to a spiritual reality—as natural surroundings often correspond to spiritual conditions—it's clear that changing our spiritual climate sets the stage for a shift in spiritual seasons. We can't shift our seasons—God does that. But we can create a climate that invites Him to do the work in our hearts that prepares us for the next season.

What is the spiritual climate over your life? If you are angry, ungrateful, complaining, angry, greedy, controlling, critical, impatient, indifferent, discouraged, jealous, frightened, frustrated, unforgiving, resentful, bitter, selfish, or something of the like, you're creating a spiritual climate over your life that repels the Holy Spirit. He loves you, yes, but your flesh is warring against His Spirit.

If, by contrast, you are thankful, peaceful, prayerful, joyful, generous, forgiving, loving, content, self-less, hopeful, faithful, inspired, worshipful, you are creating an atmosphere that attracts the presence of God. And the presence of the Holy Spirit is the ultimate key to spiritual change and growth. Put another way, we need to cultivate the fruit of the Spirit in our lives and reject the works of the flesh. In doing so, we position our hearts for God to shift us into fruitful seasons of harvest.

Wait for the Suddenlies

When you change your climate unto a season shift, it will lead to a suddenly. *Merriam-Webster* defines "suddenly" means "happening or coming unexpectedly; a changing angle or character all at once; marked by or manifesting abruptness or haste; made or brought about in a short time."

After weeks of praying in unity, "Suddenly a sound like a mighty rushing wind" and the 120 in the Upper Room were filled with the Spirit" (see Acts 2). When Paul and Barnabas experienced persecution for Christ's sake, suddenly an earthquake rose up and opened the doors to the jail (see Acts 16:26). Suddenly.

Suddenly you may shift into a promotion. Suddenly you may shift from sickness to health. Suddenly you may shift into greater authority in the spirit.

Suddenly you may shift from a dark night of the soul to greater revelation of Christ. Suddenly you may shift from feelings of oppression to new levels of freedom. Suddenly.

Believe for the suddenlies in 2018. Expect them to happen.

Wait with anticipation, but understand that you have to do your part. Like the disciples in the Upper Room, you need to pray. Like Paul and Barnabas in the prison, you need to praise.

In other words, you need to create a spiritual climate over your life that invites the Holy Spirit to work in your heart, in your life and in your circumstances. Your climate change will eventually lead to a season shift that will bring a suddenly you could never make happen in your own strength.

Take heart in Isaiah 48:3: "I have declared the former things from the beginning and they went forth from My mouth, and I announced them. Suddenly I did them, and they came to pass."

The Lord spoke to me clearly when I was in Singapore in 2017: "Expect the unexpected." When I meditated on this, He showed me many things, including sudden encounters with God. In this season, we're going to see God move in extraordinary ways. Of course, we have to position ourselves in faith to believe and receive.

Pray this prayer with me: *Father, in the name of Jesus, I come to you in all humility asking for help to walk with an awareness of You, an awareness of Your kingdom, an awareness of Your promises, an awareness of who I really am and what belongs to me in Christ, and an awareness of the forces of hell seeking to rob me of the promises You've made. Open the eyes of my heart so I can gain heaven's perspective and release the kingdom to shift atmospheres in the places you've called me to walk, in Jesus' name.*

CHAPTER 9
YOU CAN'T CHANGE YOURSELF

"You have authority. You have influence. You have power. You have an anointing."

"Behold, I will do a new thing, now it shall spring forth; shall you not know it? I will even make a road in the wilderness and rivers in the desert" (Isaiah 43:19).

That rhema word from Scripture nearly four years ago kicked off a season of change in my life that hasn't quit. I'm convinced that I've seen more changes in my life over the past few years than some people see in two decades. I'm talking major life changes. Some of those changes produced immediate joy. Others produced prolonged pain before producing joy.

I've noticed a cycle, if you can call it that, where one change comes at the heels of another and then another—finally followed by the avalanche. Some of the changes are welcomed while others are gut-wrenching, even when you know it's God's will. I still don't like change, but I've learned to embrace it because I've seen the fruit of faithfully following God through life's transitions—and that fruit is good!

Facing Sweeping Changes

Maybe you are seeing sweeping changes in your life even now or soon will as part of this metamorphosis. Whether they are welcome changes, like getting married and having a baby, or unwelcome changes, like getting divorced and losing a loved one to death, change can cause confusion, stress, delight, anticipation, fear, joy—a whole range of fickle emotions that ebb and flow with what seems like the powerful rush of a rolling tide.

Before we go any further, understand this: The only thing that doesn't change is God. Jesus Christ is the same yesterday, today and forever (see Hebrews. 13:8). Everything else—I said everything else—is subject to change. I won't recite all the words of Solomon here, but suffice it to say that "to everything there is a season, a time for every purpose under heaven" (Ecclesiastes 3:1).

So as you go through a season of change—especially gut-wrenching changes—how do you position yourself to walk worthy of your calling? How do you yield to God's will while resisting the enemy? How do you embrace the change that will produce more of the character of Christ and the fruit of the Spirit in your life—and perhaps in the lives of others involved?

Learning to Let Go

Keeping your eyes on God, who doesn't change, is the critical first step (see Hebrews 12:2). The Lord really is your rock, your fortress and your deliverer (see Psalm 18:2). His hope is the anchor of your soul (see Hebrews 6:19).

When you keep your mind on Him, you'll remain in perfect peace even amid the most stormy changes (see Isaiah 26:3). When you keep your eyes on Him, you'll find that road in the wilderness and the rivers in the desert that Isaiah prophesied (see Isaiah 43:19).

Next, you've got to be willing to let go of what the Holy Spirit is showing you to let go of. If you want that new beginning—if you want that new thing God has in store for you—then you must let go even if it feels like it's going to kill you; even if you have to do it through tears; even if other people don't agree with you; even if you can't see where to go next.

Isaiah 26:3 – You will keep in perfect peace those whose minds are steadfast, because they trust in You.

Isaiah 43:19 – See, I am doing a new thing! Now it springs up; do you not perceive it? I am making a way in the wilderness and streams in the wastelands.

When you let go, He'll show you what to do next, just like he showed Abram what to do when he left everything behind to follow God (see Genesis 12:1-3).

The letting go part is probably the hardest part of the change process. I've written several articles—including "How to Forget Those Things Which Are Behind," "Burning the Bridges to Your Past," and "Are You Willing to Leave Your Baggage Behind?"—on this topic because it's a real pain point for people.

I had to learn that lesson and learn it well, and you should too.

Sometimes there are soul ties with people, churches or even things that you need to break. The pull you feel to keep going back to the same people and things God has told you to leave behind is often a soul tie.

A soul tie is a deep emotional bond. When David met King Saul's son Jonathan, there was an immediate bond between them.

The Bible says, "The soul of Jonathan was knit to the soul of David, and Jonathan loved him as his own soul" (1 Samuel 18:1). That's intense. When you move on, sometimes you have to break soul ties, in the name of Jesus, before you can move forward full speed.

Pursuing the New Vision

Once you've let go of the people, places and things holding you back, ask God for a new vision. What does God have next for you? I assure you, He has a new thing in mind. God may even resurrect an old dream you thought was dead. You won't see this spiritual vision come to pass overnight—there is a time of transition between the old and the new—but with clarity, you'll have the discipline you need to keep pressing forward (see Proverbs 29:18).

During this metamorphosis time, pursue any emotional healing you need. We all suffer wounds from the words and actions of others, from the work of the enemy, from our own sinful mistakes, from disappointing life events and even from doing the work of the ministry. Sometimes we have to suffer for Christ (see Philippians 1:29). It's easy enough to get resentful, bitter and unforgiving. But walking toward your new beginning means letting go of these things also. Be assured that God is using it all for good (see Romans 8:28).

Many men in the Bible suffered great losses on their way to greatness. Just look at Job, Joseph and David. But all of these men endured the enemy's best shot and took back what he stole—and then some. Each of them had a new beginning that brought glory to God.

Proverbs 29:18 – Where there is no revelation; people cast off restraint; but blessed is the one who heeds wisdom's instruction.

They persevered, kept their eyes on God and waited on His deliverance. So while you are enduring gut-wrenching pain, take comfort in God's Word: "Behold, I will do a new thing, now it shall spring forth; shall you not know it? I will even make a road in the wilderness and rivers in the desert" (see Isaiah 43:19). Amen.

Yielding to the Metamorphosis

I appreciate the Dictionary.com definition of metamorphosis because it touches on witchcraft. Witchcraft is listed as a work of the flesh in Galatians 5. We cannot morph ourselves into His image. We cannot change ourselves no matter how hard we work at it.

Like clay on a potter's wheel, we must yield to the making process so God can shape and mold us into a vessel of honor for His use. We must not resist God during this metamorphosis or risk getting crushed in the hand of the potter. Consider Jeremiah's chronicle:

"The word which came to Jeremiah from the Lord, saying: 'Arise and go down to the potter's house, and there I will cause you to hear My words.' Then I went down to the potter's house, and there he was making something on the wheel. Yet the vessel that he made of clay was spoiled in the hand of the potter; so he made it again into another vessel, as seemed good to the potter to make it" (Jeremiah 18:1-4).

In this year of radical metamorphosis, we must yield so we don't miss an opportunity to realize our highest and best use for the Master. Failing to yield will bring delays and we may never reach our highest calling if we refuse to submit to what the Lord is doing in this season. He still loves us and will still use us if we miss our kairos season. Nevertheless, we don't want to be spoiled in the hand of the Potter and made into a vessel less than what He has in mind.

Much the same, we don't get to choose how the Lord morphs us. We don't get to decide who we want to be. Our Maker is our morpher. Paul confronts this reality in Roman 9:20-21: "Shall the thing formed say to him who formed it, 'Why have you made me like this?' Does the potter not have power over the clay to make from the same lump one vessel for honor and another for dishonor?"

Radical morphing means radical yielding. God may have in mind development changes that will force you to lay aside childish things for His greater purpose. Paul the apostle put it this way: "When I was a child, I spoke as a child, I understood as a child, and I thought as a child. But when I became a man, I put away childish things" (1 Corinthians 13:11).

God may require to go deeper into the Word of God to root out carnal mindsets that are holding you back from your greater purpose. Paul said, "I have fed you with milk and not with solid food. For to this day you were not able to endure it. Nor are you able now, for you are still worldly. Since there is envy, strife, and divisions among you, are you not worldly and behaving as mere men?" (1 Corinthians 5:2-3)

God wants to morph us into the image of His Son, and that demands spending time in the Word and fellowshipping with His Spirit so we can mature and begin to see things from His perspective. The writer of Hebrews put it this way:

"For though by now you should be teachers, you need someone to teach you again the first principles of the oracles of God and have come to need milk rather than solid food. Everyone who lives on milk is unskilled in the word of righteousness, for he is a baby. But solid food belongs to those who are mature, for those who through practice have powers of discernment that are trained to distinguish good from evil" (Hebrews 5:12-14).

In the prophetic word, the Lord assures: "You have authority. You have influence. You have power. You have an anointing." But He wants to increase your authority, increase your influence, increase your power and increase your anointing. You can't make this happen, but you can cooperate with the grace of God to see it happen.

Pray this prayer with me: *Father, in the name of Jesus, help me to avoid works of the flesh to change myself. I don't want to fall into the religious trap of performance-based Christianity. Give me the grace to yield to the work you are doing in my heart. Help me to embrace the changes You have ordained for me in this metamorphosis.*

CHAPTER 10
WHAT TO EXPECT IN THE
WORLD AROUND YOU

As I said at the start of this short book, prophetically I'm seeing widespread metamorphosis. I see metamorphosis in people, in companies, in churches, and in societies. The metamorphosis is coming out of an intense struggle in the hearts and minds of people. It's coming out of church splits and past moral failures in leadership. And it's coming from a changing of the guard in cities, states and nations.

Let's be clear, the metamorphosis is not guaranteed. This is the Lord's will. Just as the Great Awakening that's coming will not revolutionize every person in every nation of the world, not everyone will enter into this metamorphosis process. Some will reject God's plans for their lives, companies, churches, cities and nations. Some will yield to a demonic metamorphosis and will work to oppose God's will.

To be sure, the battle between good and evil will continue until Jesus comes back, but Jesus is coming sooner than many may think. I don't know when He will return, but I know His Second Coming is one day closer than it was yesterday. A metamorphosis is underway and will continue, at some level, until ultimate metamorphosis when the Lord cracks the sky. We will be changed in the twinkling of an eye (see 1 Corinthians 15:52). We'll witness a new heaven and a new earth (see Revelation 21:1).

The World Is Changing Faster Than Ever
As I pen this in late 2017, it's apparent that the world has morphed and is morphing. In July 2017, *Bloomberg* declared, "The World is About to Change Even Faster" in a news article about how the pace of innovation and disruption is accelerating.

Indeed, we are in an age of innovation and acceleration. Prophetically speaking, as part of this metamorphosis I see a spirit of innovation coming into the church. The see innovations throughout the Bible in the form of inventions, which are tied to our creator God's wisdom impartations. Proverbs 8:12 tells us, "I wisdom dwell with prudence, and find out knowledge of witty inventions."

The Bible speaks of Jubal, the first of those who played the harp and flute (see Genesis 4:21) and Zillah, the forger of all instruments of bronze and iron (see Genesis 4:22). Second Chronicles 26:15 speaks of Uriah who made engines of war invented by skillful men.

In modern times, many inventors credit God with their innovations. George Washington Carver, who invented at least 300 products from peanuts—including paper, soap, glue, and medicines—said, "The Lord has guided me," and "without my Savior, I am nothing." Mary Hunter, an award-winning chef, insists all her recipes come from heaven: "I don't have a cookbook. God gives me my own. Prayer is where I get 99 percent of my recipes."

Gary Starkweather, an engineer who invented the laser printer, said: "I believe that to a great extent, the creativity we possess is because the Creator put it there. God put things [in us] as tool developers and creative individuals and I think it has to please Him when He sees us use those faculties to make something completely new."

I agree with Starkweather's revelation and we need to embrace this pure wisdom from above. God is a Creator, an Innovator and an Inventor and we were created in His image and in His likeness.

John 1:3 proclaims, "All things were created through Him, and without Him nothing was created that was created." I believe this is still true; and that witty inventions, technologies, scientific breakthroughs and other innovations that make a positive impact on society are inspired by His Spirit, even if the inventor does not yet know Him.

The church has been lagging on the innovation front. Religion has offered us a form of godliness without its power (see Timothy 3:5). When the power of God comes on the scene, eyes are opened to what was unseen, dreams come alive, and creativity is inspired. The Lord wants to bring a metamorphosis to the church that is innovation-driven so we can reach unchurched people who have rejected religion.

Accelerated Acceleration

Part of this metamorphosis, which will begin even now and continue in the years ahead, will see an accelerated acceleration. Accelerate means "to move faster: to gain speed; to progress from grade to grade more rapidly than usual; to bring about at an earlier time; to cause to move faster; to hasten the progress or development of," according to *Merriam-Webster*. Acceleration means "a change in velocity," according to Dictionary.com.

We're about to those who accept their God-given callings and embrace the metamorphosis move faster, gain speed, progress more rapidly and step into the new anointings at a younger age. Millennials are poised for a rapid rise. Part of this prophesied accelerated acceleration is pressing into the spirit of innovation and creativity. The two are tied together.

At the same time, for the older generation, God is going to make up for lost time and fulfill Joel 2:25-32 as they embrace the spirit of innovation: "So I will restore to you the years that the swarming locust has eaten, the crawling locust, the consuming locust, and the chewing locust, my great army which I sent among you. You shall eat in plenty and be satisfied, and praise the name of the Lord your God, Who has dealt wondrously with you; and My people shall never be put to shame."

The struggle of metamorphosis at the individual level is not always a physical one. Many times it's the challenge to embrace something new—that new wineskin for the new wine God wants to pour into you and release through you. Sometimes the struggle—the suffering—is a pruning away of relationships that you have to let go because some are not called or simply are not willing to go with you to the next level.

A Demonic Metamorphosis

Remember one of the Dictionary.com definitions of metamorphosis is "a complete change in form, structure, or substance, as transformation by magic or witchcraft." While the Lord is working to morph people, churches and society at large, the enemy is organizing a counterfeit move. Instead of innovation, perversion is his ploy. Instead of accelerating toward God's glory, he is accelerating darkness. His propaganda is rising.

Watching old videos of healing evangelists like Kathryn Kuhlman, A.A. Allen, Jack Coe and Oral Roberts is one of my favorite things to do. In the last few months alone, I've consumed hundreds of hours of videos showing the miracle-working power of God and bold revival preaching that makes no apologies for the Rock of Offense.

While watching an A.A. Allen miracle reel my ears perked up when I heard the late Brother Allen declare a revival of the devil's witchcraft. Of course, this was back in the 1950s. What was a revival of witchcraft then has turned into a full-blown movement.

"An awful lot of people are sick, diseased and afflicted under a curse, under a spell because of the present revival of witchcraft around the world," Allen declared. "There has never been a time in history when there has been such a devil's revival of witchcraft."

Think about it for a minute. In Allen's day, there was no such thing as Harry Potter. Allen made this declaration before popular TV shows like Bewitched, Charmed and The Witches of East End—and before films like Rosemary's Baby, The Blair Witch Project and Season of the Witch. Indeed, it was before children's media like Meg and Mog, The Witch Family and Witches in Stitches hit the mainstream.

A Revival of the Devil's Witchcraft

We've seen the devil pressing hard to bring witchcraft deeper into our schools, our homes and our entertainment venues. We reported on how a new witchcraft-inspired challenge is luring kids into summoning demons. It's called Charlie Charlie and it's sweeping the nation and the world under the guise of a carefree fortune-telling game. Faith leaders are sounding the alarm.

I wrote about a new devil-inspired show called Lucifer on, of all stations, Fox. "Bored and unhappy as the lord of hell, Lucifer Morningstar has abandoned his throne and retired to L.A., where he owns Lux, an upscale nightclub," the show's description reads. "Charming, charismatic and devilishly handsome, Lucifer is enjoying his retirement, indulging in a few of his favorite things—wine, women and song—when a beautiful pop star is brutally murdered outside of Lux."

Meanwhile, theaters in Miami are putting on a play based on John Van Druten's Bell, Book and Candle, which is about a witch who puts a love spell on a publisher who is soon to be engaged to his sweetheart. Of one of her albums, Florence and The Machine singer Florence Welch says she "got into obsessing about the LA witchcraft scene, and I was imagining this concept album about a witch trial in Hollywood, and someone falls in love."

I'm believing for a Third Great Awakening. But the devil is clearly driving toward a great awakening of the occult. This revival of the devil's witchcraft is unto an awakening to the occult that will set the very elect up to be deceived, it if is possible (see Matt. 24:24). False signs and wonders will rise, along with false prophets and false christs.

As you may know, I've written a book dealing with spiritual witchcraft called *Satan's Deadly Trio: Defeating the Deceptions of Jezebel, Witchcraft and Religion.* Many times, infirmities are rooted in the devil's witchcraft—and sometimes it comes from the spirit of Jezebel. The Bible talks about Jezebel and her witchcrafts (see 2 Kings 9:22). Witchcraft can't heal you, but it can release confusion, sickness and disease, depression and other ailments. At our recent women's conference, Jesus healed 23 ladies—and several of them were afflicted with witchcraft.

—

We need to pray. A generation of youth has been exposed to witchcraft games, television shows, movies and more. The enemy is seducing people who are looking for the supernatural into a counterfeit movement could have dangerous eternal outcomes. In the book of Revelation, God has made it clear the fate of those who practice such things: sorcerers will have their portion in the lake that burns with fire and brimstone (see Revelation 21:8). Let's keep pressing back this darkness.

The opposition will be great for those standing for God's purposes in this season, but His sufficient grace will help those who refuse to bow to the false gods in the seven mountains to prevail. A prevailing spirit will rest of the pioneers of metamorphosis in the seven mountains of society. Glory will rest upon those who are willing to endure persecution for the sake of the gospel. Those who give voice to the gospel will see provision amid the persecution from unlikely places as a measure of the wealth transfer we've heard about so long manifests.

There truly is a revival of the devil's witchcraft, as Allen put it, and it's far darker today than it was in his time. The good news is Isaiah 60:1-3 is true:

"Arise, shine; For your light has come! And the glory of the Lord is risen upon you. For behold, the darkness shall cover the earth, and deep darkness the people; But the Lord will arise over you, and His glory will be seen upon you. The Gentiles shall come to your light, and kings to the brightness of your rising."

Change Begins With You

The direction we head is largely up to the church—and the church is made up of people. We can't see a great awakening until we see individuals wake up. Revival begins with you. Change begins with you.

We yearn to see signs, wonders and miracles manifest today as they did in the Book of Acts, don't we? But are we willing to pay the price the early church paid? Are we willing to die to self? Are we willing to relinquish control to the Holy Spirit so He can move like He wants to move? Are we willing to repent for the character flaws that hold us back? Are we willing to walk in love and unity with true believers who don't believe exactly the same as we do? Are we willing to war against the spirit of compromise that is raging against the church in this age? Revival begins with you.

The Book of Acts never fails to fascinate me. It is the Holy Ghost in action, the gifts of the Spirit made manifest, a charismatic believer's delight. Indeed, many of us want to see the Holy Ghost move in the church—and in the world—like that again. Well, I beseech you to consider these four words: Revival begins with you.

Sure, we see a ration of revival spring up from time to time. We see a measure of the miraculous. We see demons cast out, in the name of Jesus. But it doesn't compare to the book of Acts, does it? Revival begins with you.

Despite 24/7 prayer movements that bear plenty of fruit, we don't see people waiting to stand in our shadows hoping to get healed. Despite the apostolic movement (and the thousands of Christians who call themselves apostles), we rarely see people raised from the dead.

Despite large stadiums of sincere people repenting in tears before the Lord for the sins of generations, we are yet a far cry from the reality of the book of Acts. Revival begins with you.

We can't do the Lord's part—we can't force miracles, signs and wonders. But we can do our part—we can tear down the strongholds in our own souls that are preventing us from walking in the fullness of the Spirit.

We can stop tolerating spirits that tempt us to sin. We can start interceding for the fallen saints instead of playing judge.

In other words, we can start living like the saints lived in the book of Acts: sold out, on fire and ready to die for the gospel. Revival begins with you.

Again, we can't manufacture miracles. We can't work up wonders. But we can cooperate with the Holy Spirit to separate the profane from the holy in our own hearts and in our own minds. We can purge ourselves and lay aside every weight that holds us back. We can allow the Spirit of God to do a deep work in us and so the Spirit of God can do a great work through us. Revival begins with you—and me.

I've discovered we cannot set ourselves on fire. Not really. God is the ultimate fire-starter. But we can position our hearts close to His burning flame of love and catch His fire as the wind of the Holy Spirit blows it in our direction. We can't do God's part, but God won't do our part.

So if revival begins with you—and me— where does that leave us? Waiting on the Lord, but not in the way we have been. The Hebrew word for "wait" in the context of waiting on the Lord is "qavah." It is active verb that means to wait, look for, hope, expect; to wait or look eagerly for; to lie in wait for; and to wait for, linger for. We need to wait like we expect Him to show up.

1. Look for the promise. Jacob went into a downward spiral after he thought Joseph was ripped apart by lions. He was never quite the same after he lost Joseph. When he heard Joseph was alive, his spirit stirred but when he saw the wagons that Joseph sent to bring him back to Egypt for the grand family reunion in the midst of a famine, the spirit of Jacob revived (Gen. 45:27). Look at the promises of revival God has given through prophetic words. Look at the scriptural incidents of revival and deliverance. Look for the promises of God and be revived.

2. Drink from living water. The Bible is the inspired Word of God, but with a Word famine rising in the land and the nearly-constant spiritual warfare raging, many are thirsty for a rhema word of God—a true Holy Spirit-inspired prophecy that flows like a river of living water. After Samson struck down 1,000 men with the jawbone of an ass, he was thirsty.

"'You gave this great deliverance through Your servant, but now may I die of thirst and fall into the hands of the uncircumcised?' So God split open the basin at Lehi, and water flowed out of it. He drank, was refreshed, and revived" (Judges 15:18-19).

The living water God provides revived Samson—and it will revival us.

3. Stay humble. God resists the proud. He does not revive them. He gives grace, exalts and revives the humble and repentant. Walking in a revival lifestyle means walking in a repentance lifestyle—we need to be quick to repent when we've missed the mark.

"For thus says the High and Lofty One who inhabits eternity, whose name is Holy: I dwell in the high and holy place and also with him who is of a contrite and humble spirit, to revive the spirit of the humble, and to revive the heart of the contrite ones" (Isaiah 57:15).

4. Pray for personal revival. When the son of the widow of Zarephath died, her response to Elijah showed she connected this death to sin, but Elijah knew better. He knew it was not the Lord's will for the boy to die. Elijah took him out of her arms of unbelief and despair and into his arms of faith. Elijah set out to pray.

"He cried to the Lord and said, 'O Lord, my God, have You brought tragedy upon the widow with whom I live by killing her son?' And he stretched himself upon the child three times and cried to the Lord and said, 'O Lord, my God, I pray that You let this child's soul come into him again.' He Lord heard the voice of Elijah, and the soul of the child came into him again, and he was revived. Elijah took the child and brought him down out of the chamber into the house and returned him to his mother, and Elijah said, "See, your son lives!" (1 Kings 17:20-23).

In order to revive that which looks dead, we need to stop looking at the outward condition, which stirs unbelief and despair, and pray until we see God's will come to pass.

The psalmists prayed revival prayers. In these prayers, the word "revive" is from the Hebrew word "chayah," which means "to live, have life, remain alive, sustain life, live prosperously, live forever, be quickened, be alive, be restored to life or health." It also means to restore and cause to grow. Consider these verses:

Psalm 71:20: "You who have shown me great distresses and troubles will revive me again, and will bring me up again from the depths of the earth."

Psalm 85:6: "Will You not revive us again, that Your people may rejoice in You?"

Psalm 119:25: "My soul clings to the dust; revive me according to Your word."

Psalm 119:37: "Turn away my eyes from beholding worthlessness, and revive me in Your way."

Psalm 119:40: "Behold, I have a longing for Your precepts; revive me in Your righteousness."

Psalm 119:50: "This is my comfort in my affliction, for Your word revives me."

Psalm 119:88: "Revive me according to Your lovingkindness, that I may keep the testimony from Your mouth."

Psalm 119:93: "I will never forget Your precepts, for with them You have revived me."

Psalm 119:107: "I am greatly afflicted; revive me, O Lord, according to Your word."

Psalm 119:149: "Hear my voice according to Your lovingkindness, O Lord; revive me according to Your judgment."

Psalm 119:154: "Plead my cause, and defend me; revive me according to Your word."

Psalm 119:156: "Great are Your compassions, O Lord; revive me according to Your judgments."

Psalm 119:159: "Consider how I love Your precepts; revive me, O Lord, according to Your lovingkindness."

Psalm 143:11: "Revive me, O Lord, for Your name's sake, for Your righteousness' sake bring my soul out of trouble."

5. *Believe God will answer.* When we pray, we're supposed to pray in faith, nothing waivering. James says a double-minded man is unstable in all his ways and should not expect to receive anything from God (see James 1:8). Habakkuk prayed to God, believed for an answer—and got one:

Habakkuk 3:1-3: "A prayer of Habakkuk the prophet, on Shigionoth. O Lord, I have heard the report of You, and was afraid; O Lord, revive Your work in the midst of the years! In the midst of these years make them known; in wrath remember mercy. God came from Teman, and the Holy One from Mount Paran. Selah His glory covered the heavens, and the earth was full of His praise."

A Metamorphosis is Underway

I'll prophesy it once more: A metamorphosis is underway. Romans 8:19 tells us "For [even the whole] creation (all nature) waits expectantly and longs earnestly for God's sons to be made known [waits for the revealing, the disclosing of their sonship]."

Indeed, the earth itself is even morphing. NASA released images in January 2017 showing "dramatic shifts" in the sizes of forests, ice cover and water levels over the past four decades. Namely, they are shrinking.

"Some document the effects of urbanization or the ravage of natural hazards such as fires and floods," NASA says. "All show our planet in a state of flux."

Our planet is in a state of flux. Nations are in a state of flux. The church is in a state of flux. Well, the world calls it flux. The Lord is calling it metamorphosis.

[1]https://www.fastcompany.com/1680127/8-ways-the-world-will-change-by-2052

ABOUT JENNIFER LECLAIRE

Jennifer LeClaire is an internationally recognized author, apostolic-prophetic voice to her generation, and conference speaker. She carries a reforming voice that inspires and challenges believers to pursue intimacy with God, cultivate their spiritual gifts and walk in the fullness of what God has called them to do. Jennifer is contending for awakening in the nations through intercession and spiritual warfare, strong apostolic preaching and practical prophetic teaching that equips the saints for the work of the ministry.

Jennifer is senior leader of Awakening House of Prayer in Fort Lauderdale, FL, founder of the Ignite Network and founder of the Awakening Blaze prayer movement.

Jennifer formerly served as the first-ever editor of *Charisma* magazine. Her work also appeared in a Charisma House book entitled *Understanding the Five-Fold Ministry* which offers a biblical study to uncover the true purpose for the fivefold ministry and *The Spiritual Warfare Bible*, which is designed to help you use the Bible to access the power of the Holy Spirit against demonic strongholds and activity. Some of Jennifer's work is also archived in the Flower Pentecostal Heritage Museum.

Jennifer is a prolific author who has written over 25 books, including *The Heart of the Prophetic*, *A Prophet's Heart, Fervent Faith, Did the Spirit of God Say That? 27 Keys to Judging Prophecy, Breakthrough!*, and *Doubtless: Faith that Overcomes the World*. Some of her materials have been translated into Spanish and Korean.

Jennifer's other titles include: *The Spiritual Warrior's Guide to Defeating Jezebel*; *Developing Faith for the Working of Miracles; The Making of a Prophet; Mornings With the Holy Spirit: Listening Daily to the Still Small Voice of God* and *The Next Great Move of God: An Appeal to Heaven for Spiritual Awakening.*

Beyond her frequent appearances on the Elijah List, Jennifer writes one of *Charisma*'s most popular prophetic columns, The Plumb Line, and frequently contributes to *Charisma*'s Prophetic Insight newsletter. Her media ministry includes her website; 500,000 followers on Facebook, Twitter and YouTube, Jennifer has been interviewed on numerous media outlets including USA Today, BBC, CBN, The Alan Colmes Show, Bill Martinez Live, Babbie's House, Atlanta Live and Sid Roth's It's Supernatural, as well as serving as an analyst for Rolling Thunder Productions on a *Duck Dynasty* special presentation.

Jennifer also sits on the media advisory board of the Hispanic Israel Leadership Coalition.

Jennifer is affiliated with:

Network Ekklessia International, an apostolic network founded by Dutch Sheets;

Forerunner Ministries, founded by Ken Malone;

Bill Hamon's Christian International Network;

Chuck Pierce's apostolic network

USCAL, the United States Coalition of Apostolic Leaders;

The International Society of Deliverance Ministers

Jennifer has a powerful testimony of God's power to set the captives free and claim beauty for ashes. She shares her story with women who need to understand the love and grace of God in a lost and dying world. Click here for a personal Q&A with Jennifer.

Click here to read Jennifer's endorsements.

You can also learn more about Jennifer in this broadcast on Sid Roth's *It's Supernatural.*

OTHER BOOKS BY JENNIFER LECLAIRE

Angels on Assignment Again
Releasing the Angels of Abundant Harvest
The Heart of the Prophetic
A Prophet's Heart
The Making of a Prophet
The Spiritual Warrior's Guide to Defeating Jezebel
Did the Spirit of God Say That?
Satan's Deadly Trio
Jezebel's Puppets
The Spiritual Warfare Battle Plan
Waging Prophetic Warfare
Dream Wild!
Faith Magnified
Fervent Faith
Breakthrough!
Mornings With the Holy Spirit
Evenings With the Holy Spirit
Revival Hubs Rising
The Next Great Move of God
Developing Faith for the Working of Miracles

You can download Jennifer's mobile apps by searching for "Jennifer LeClaire" in your app store and find Jennifer's podcasts on iTunes.

I believe in prophetic ministry with every fiber of my being, but we all know the prophetic movement has seen its successes and failures. With an end times army of prophets and prophetic people rising up according to Joel 2:28 and Acts 2:17-20, it's more important than ever that we equip the saints for the work of prophetic ministry.

Enter Ignite.

Ignite is a prophetic network birthed out of an encounter with the Lord that set a fire in my hearts to raise up a generation of prophets and prophetic people who flow accurately, operate in integrity, and pursue God passionately. I am laboring to cultivate a family of apostolic and prophetic voices and companies of prophets in the nations who can edify, comfort and exhort each other as we contend for pure fire in the next great move of God. My vision for Ignite covers the spiritual, educational, relational and accountability needs of five-fold ministers and intercessory prayer leaders.

You can learn more at **http://www.ignitenow.org/**.

AWAKENING BLAZE PRAYER MOVEMENT

The Awakening Blaze mission in any city is to draw a diverse group of intercessors who have one thing in common: to contend for the Lord's will in its city, state and nation.

The vision of Awakening Blaze prayer spokes is to unite intercessors in cities across the nations of the earth to cooperate with the Spirit of God to see the second half of 2 Chronicles 7:14—"If My people, who are called by My name, will humble themselves and pray, and seek My face and turn from their wicked ways, then I will hear from heaven, and will forgive their sin and will heal their land"—come to pass.

For many years, intercessors have been repenting, praying, and seeking God for strategies. Awakening Blaze intercessors will press into see the land healed, souls saved, churches established, ministries launched, and other Spirit-driven initiatives. Blaze intercessors will help undergird other ministries in their city, partnering with them in prayer where intercession may be lacking. Although Awakening Blaze prayer spokes are not being planted to birth churches, it is possible that churches could spring up from these intercessory prayer cells if the Lord wills.

You can find out more about this prayer movement at **http://www.awakeningblaze.com/**.

Made in the USA
Lexington, KY
30 December 2017